USBORNE GUIDE TO
UNDERSTANDING THE
MICRO

Judy Tatchell and Bill Bennett
Edited by Lisa Watts

S0-AIJ-878

This book was designed by Round Designs and Roger Priddy and illustrated by Tim Cowdell, Graham Round, Jeremy Banks, Graham Smith, Martin Newton, Ian Stephen, Kuo Kang Chen and Martin Salisbury.

Contents

2

About this book

This book is for anyone who wants to know about microcomputers. It shows what you can do with them, how you use them, and how they work. It explains computer jargon so you can go on to read and understand more about computers.

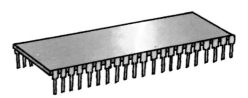

Microcomputers are small, multi-purpose computers. You can play games on them, draw pictures and sometimes even make sounds and music. They can also do complicated sums very quickly, and you can keep diaries and catalogues of records and slides, or anything else you collect.

The first part of the book explains how to use a micro and how you give it a program telling it what to do. There is an introduction to writing programs in BASIC, which is the programming language most micros understand, and there are lots of programming hints. If you have access to a micro, there are some games programs you can try out.

The book then describes how a micro works, and how it makes pictures and different sounds. It shows the inside of a micro with its tiny silicon chips which do all the processing. You can also find out how some micros can be linked to other computers thousands of miles away to bring all sorts of information into your own home. Micros can be used to control robots, or other electronic equipment, such as model railways, too.

Although to begin with you only need an ordinary television set to use with a micro, you can buy lots of other pieces of equipment to connect to it – a light pen for drawing pictures directly on the screen, for instance, or special attachments for using with arcade-type games. The book describes these, too.

At the end of the book there is a guide to buying a micro. It tells you about some of the most popular home computers so you can compare them and explains the terminology used to describe a computer.

Meet the micro

These two pages show a micro and how to set it up. Not all micros look exactly like the one in the picture. Most home computers, though, consist of a keyboard that you connect to a TV. Some micros have screens specially designed for them. These are called visual display units (VDUs), or monitors. All new micros are supplied with manuals to tell you how to use them. Before setting up a micro, check its manual for special instructions.

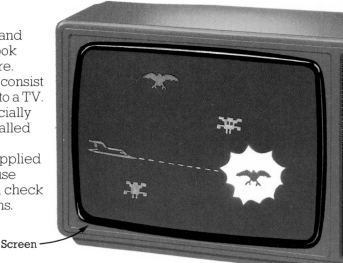

Screen

Keyboard
You give the micro instructions and information by typing on the keyboard.

Keyboard

Sockets where leads from the TV and the mains plug into the micro.

All the important parts of the micro are kept inside the keyboard, where it does its work.

Where the micro does its work

The micro has an electronic memory where it stores information and instructions.

Input

Output

The "brain" of the micro is usually inside the keyboard. It consists of a central processing unit (CPU) which does all the work, and a memory. Before it can do anything the CPU needs a set of instructions called a program. This is stored in the memory along with the information, or data, you want it to work on. Programs and data are called input. The results are called output.

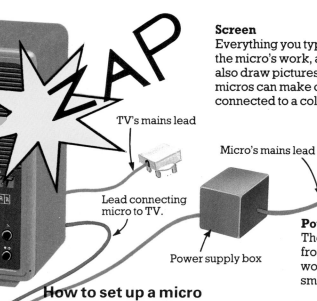

Screen

Everything you type on the keyboard, and the results of the micro's work, appear on the screen. The micro can also draw pictures and make shapes on the screen. Most micros can make coloured pictures if they are connected to a colour TV.

TV's mains lead

Micro's mains lead

Some micros can produce music and sound effects.

Lead connecting micro to TV.

Power supply box

Power supply

The power supply box reduces the power from the mains to a level the micro can work on, and keeps the power supply smooth.

How to set up a micro

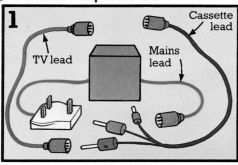

1

TV lead

Cassette lead

Mains lead

Most micros have three leads, one to link the keyboard to a TV, one to plug the keyboard into the mains electricity supply, and a third to connect it to a cassette recorder.*

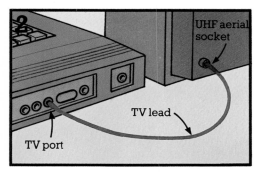

2

UHF aerial socket

TV lead

TV port

To connect the keyboard to a TV, pull the aerial plug out of the TV. Then plug one end of the micro's TV lead into the hole marked TV on the keyboard and the other into the UHF socket on the TV.

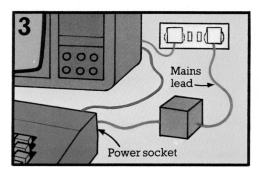

3

Mains lead

Power socket

Plug one end of the mains lead into the power socket on the keyboard and the other end into the mains at the wall. Make sure the TV is also plugged in, then switch them both on.

4

READY

Select a TV channel which you are not using for TV programmes. Tune the TV until the micro's "ready" signal appears on the screen. These signals vary from micro to micro.

5

*You use the cassette recorder to store programs for the micro. This is explained on page 16.

Programming a micro

Whether you want to use your micro to play a space game or simply to add some numbers together, you have to give it a program of instructions to tell it what to do. There are special computer languages for writing programs. They consist of words and symbols the computer can recognize and convert into its own electronic code, called machine code. Program instructions are stored in the computer's memory and then carried out by the CPU. Programs and data which you give the micro are called computer software. Parts of the micro that you can touch, like the keyboard and the screen, are called computer hardware.

1 Telling a computer what to do

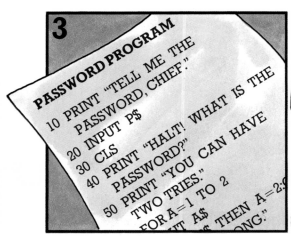

A computer can only carry out a task if it is told exactly what to do in the right order. This program tells a robot with a computer brain how to paint a window.

2

The program would not work as there is no instruction telling the robot to pick up the paint pot and brush before climbing the ladder. The robot only does what it is told to do.

3

This is part of a program* in BASIC, the language most micros use. A computer contains a set of instructions called an interpreter which translates the programming language into machine code.

4

All the work inside the computer is done in machine code. Each "word" of the code consists of patterns of pulses in the electric current flowing round the computer.

*This program is printed out in full on page 12.

The computer's memory

A computer has two kinds of memory. One is a permanent store of instructions which tell it how to work. The other is an empty memory where your program and data for a job are stored temporarily. Each time the micro is switched off, the memory empties again.

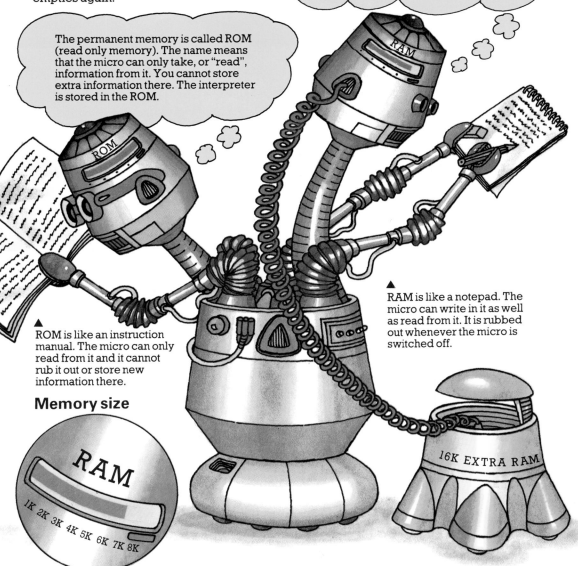

The temporary memory is called RAM (random access memory). It is sometimes called a read/write memory. Everything you put into the micro is stored or "written" in here for you to "read" or refer to, and you can also change it.

The permanent memory is called ROM (read only memory). The name means that the micro can only take, or "read", information from it. You cannot store extra information there. The interpreter is stored in the ROM.

▲ RAM is like a notepad. The micro can write in it as well as read from it. It is rubbed out whenever the micro is switched off.

▲ ROM is like an instruction manual. The micro can only read from it and it cannot rub it out or store new information there.

Memory size

Micros come with different sized memories. Memory size is measured by the number of machine code "words" that can be stored. Each code word is called a byte and 1024 bytes are called a kilobyte, or 1K.

One kilobyte is about the same as 500 BASIC words or symbols. It is enough to store simple programs. More advanced programs are longer and might need 8K or 16K of RAM. You can buy extra RAM, called add-on RAM packs, for most micros.

7

Looking at the keyboard

The keyboard of a micro usually looks much like a typewriter keyboard. It has the same letters and numbers, arranged in the same order. A micro also has some extra keys, though, for giving special commands in BASIC. The micro receives different electrical messages from each key. If you type in something the micro does not recognize, a message telling you so will appear on the screen saying "Error" or "Mistake". Everything you type is stored in the micro's temporary memory (RAM), and also displayed on the screen for you to check. These two pages show two different keyboards.

Letter keys
On most computers you type in a program using the symbol keys and spelling out the words with the letter keys.

Shift key and shift lock

This is the computer's multiplication sign.

Other micros might have some different keys.

Space bar
You press this to get a space between words or symbols.

Using the shift key

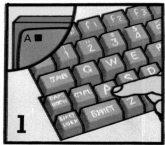

1
Most micros automatically make capital letters on the screen and cannot make small letters.

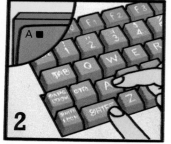

2
Some micros, though, make small letters. To make a capital letter, you hold the shift key down while you press the letter key.

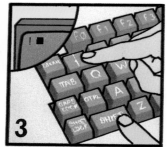

3
Where there are two symbols on the same key, you use the shift key to get the top one. Pressing a key without the shift key gives the lower one.

Programmable keys
These are special keys which you can program yourself to do special jobs such as producing certain colours each time they are pressed. Not all micros have these keys.

The figure zero on a computer usually has a stroke through it to distinguish it from the capital letter O.

The cursor is a little marker that moves across the screen as you type, to show where the next letter will appear.

If you want to change or delete something, you can move the cursor back over your typing using the cursor control keys.

Cursor control keys

Return key
At the end of each line of the program you press this key to start a new line. It also enters the line you have just typed into the micro's memory. It is sometimes called NEWLINE or ENTER.

Another micro

This keyboard is about a quarter of the size of the keyboard on the left. The design of the typing area can determine the size and shape of a micro, as the parts inside are very small. Also, there is usually room on the keyboard for sockets into which you can plug extra things like a printer or a cassette recorder. These are described later in the book.

Delete key
You can rub out mistakes you have typed using this key. On some micros it is called RUBOUT or ERASE.

This kind of micro has calculator-like keys which do not move much when you press them. Most of the keys carry complete BASIC words so you do not have to spell them out letter by letter. The keys have words, letters and symbols on them, and there are two different shift keys for selecting which message you want from a key.

9

Programs for the micro

You can buy programs in magazines, books, recorded on cassette tape or disk – or you can learn to write your own. Programs printed out line by line are called listings. Programs on cassette can be loaded into a micro using a cassette recorder. The program must be written in the correct language for the micro. This is usually BASIC, but there are several different "dialects" with different commands. The program will not work if the dialect is wrong or if it has a mistake.

What you can buy

You can buy all kinds of games programs from arcade-type games with colour pictures and exciting sound effects to more traditional ones like chess.

Where to get programs

You can buy microcomputer magazines containing listings at most newsagents. Some are produced specifically for one kind of micro. Others have programs for several different micros.

Another quite cheap way of getting programs is to buy collections of them in books. These are usually games programs written for one particular micro.

Often the programs in magazines have not been thoroughly tested and contain mistakes, called "bugs", which stop the programs working. Programs in books are usually more reliable.

Typing in listings helps you get to know BASIC and you learn to spot bugs and adapt programs if the dialect is wrong for your micro.

Prestel TV

ROM cartridges

You can sometimes get programs displayed on your TV screen. Your TV needs to be a special one that can be linked by telephone to a Viewdata system, like Prestel. These are computerized information centres. You choose which page of information you want shown.

For some micros you can buy programs in cartridges like these. You plug the cartridge into the micro and the program is automatically loaded into the micro's memory.

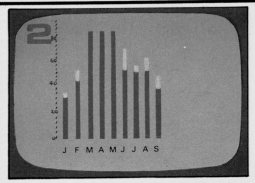

You can organize your home life with programs for keeping accounts and diaries, as well as catalogues for things you collect. These are simpler versions of programs used in business.

Educational programs can help with all kinds of learning, from spelling and maths to speaking a foreign language. Pictures on the screen often help make things clear and more interesting.

HINTS

1. Make sure the program is written in the dialect of BASIC understood by the micro you are using.

2. As a rough guide, 1K of memory is enough for about 40 program lines.

3. If a program on tape or disk that should be suitable for the micro does not work, write and tell the suppliers.

User groups

User groups provide an opportunity to meet other people interested in micros and to exchange programs and ideas. You can find out if there is one in your area by writing to a micro magazine, or look at the lists of societies at your local library.

Floppy disks

You can buy programs recorded on cassette, for which you need a cassette player. You can also buy them on floppy disk. These are made from the same material as cassette tapes, but are more expensive and you need a disk drive to use them. Shops and mail order companies sell cassettes and disks. You can find the names of suppliers in micro magazines and write off for catalogues.

Writing your own programs

Most micros are designed to understand BASIC, which is a good, general-purpose programming language. There are lots of other languages, though, and some people think Pascal is better. There are two programs in BASIC on this page. BASIC consists of symbols and words, and is quite easy to learn. The best way to start is to read lots of programs and it helps if you have a micro to try them out on. Most micros' manuals explain BASIC. You can also buy books on how to program, or you can get instruction courses on tape or disk to run on a micro.

You can find out what some BASIC terms mean in the Password Program on the right. This program is to stop spies infiltrating a secret society . . .

PASSWORD PROGRAM

```
10 PRINT "TELL ME THE PASSWORD
   CHIEF."
20 INPUT P$
30 CLS
40 PRINT "HALT! WHAT IS THE
   PASSWORD?"
50 PRINT "YOU CAN HAVE TWO
   TRIES."
60 FOR A=1 TO 2
70 INPUT A$
80 IF A$=P$ THEN A=2:GOTO 130
90 PRINT "WRONG."
100 NEXT A
110 PRINT "OUT! YOU MUST BE A SPY!"
120 END
130 PRINT "ENTER, FRIEND."
140 END
```

Each line of the program is numbered. The numbers usually go up in tens so you can insert extra lines into the program later, if necessary, without having to renumber all of them. The micro follows the program in <u>strict number order</u>.

To use, or run, the program, you type it out exactly as it is here. At the end of each line you press the key called RETURN (or ENTER or NEWLINE on some micros). Then you type RUN and the micro will carry out the program.

1 Building a program

You are testing a friend's go-kart. The steering fails as you are heading for a duckpond. The brake can be operated only by typing a special code letter which your friend forgot to tell you. There is time for five guesses at the letter before you get a soaking.

2

1. Print title and instructions
2. Choose random letter
3. Ask player for a guess at the letter
4. If guess is correct, print message and stop
5. If there is time, give hint and go back to 3
6. If not, print SPLASH and stop

The first stage in writing a program is to write down a detailed outline for the program in English. This outline is for a computer game.

Then break the idea down into steps and work out what the computer must do at each stage. List the steps in the correct order.

PRINT tells the micro to display everything inside the quotes on the screen.

INPUT tells it to expect a message from you and store it in a place in its memory called P$.

$ represents a "string" of characters.

CLS clears the screen.

FOR ... TO tells the micro how many times to carry out the instructions in lines 60 to 100.

IF ... THEN tells the micro what to do IF a certain condition is true. In this case, GOTO tells it to jump to line 130. If the condition is not true, the micro carries on to line 90.

END tells the micro it has done all it has to do and the program is finished.

```
HALT! WHAT IS THE PASSWORD?

YOU CAN HAVE TWO TRIES.

?EGGANDCHIPS

WRONG.

?MICROCHIPS

ENTER, FRIEND
```

When you run the program, the micro asks you for the password and stores it in its memory. Then it asks for a guess at the password. The word INPUT in line 70 makes a question mark on the screen to show the micro is waiting for a message from you. It compares the guess with the word in its memory and if it is the same it prints ENTER, FRIEND.

3
```
10  PRINT "SPLASH GAME"
20  PRINT
30  PRINT "THE STEERING ON THE"
40  PRINT "GOKART HAS FAILED AND"
50  PRINT "YOU ARE HEADING FOR THE"
60  PRINT "DUCKPOND. YOU MUST"
70  PRINT " PRESS THE RIGHT LETTER"
80  PRINT " TO WORK THE BRAKES."
90  PRINT "YOU HAVE 5 CHANCES."
100 LET C$=CHR$(64+INT(RND(1)*26+1))
110 FOR G=1 TO 5
120 INPUT G$
130 IF G$=C$ THEN G=5: GOTO 210
140 IF G$<C$ THEN PRINT "AFTER";
150 IF G$>C$ THEN PRINT "BEFORE";
160 PRINT G$
170 NEXT G
180 PRINT "SPLAAAAAAASH"
190 PRINT "YOU HAVE GOT WET."
200 END
210 PRINT "SCREEEEEEEECH ..."
220 PRINT "YOU STOPPED IN TIME."
230 END
```

These programs will not work on all micros because of the different dialects of BASIC. The most likely commands to need changing are CLS which tells the micro to clear the screen, and RND which tells it to pick a random number. If you have a micro and the program does not work, look in the manual to find how to alter it.

4
```
SPLASH GAME

THE STEERING ON THE
GOKART HAS FAILED AND
YOU ARE HEADING FOR THE
DUCKPOND. YOU MUST
PRESS THE RIGHT LETTER
TO WORK THE BRAKES.
YOU HAVE 5 CHANCES.
?T
BEFORE T
?R
SCREEEEEEEECH ...
YOU STOPPED IN TIME.
```

Now translate each step of the program into BASIC. Type it into the micro line by line, checking the lines to make sure they are correct.

This is what happens when you run the program. The letters after the question marks are your guesses. There is more about running programs over the page.

Running programs

When you type in a listing, all the lines of the program go into the micro's memory. Instead of typing, you can "load" a program, that is, put it into the micro by using a cassette recorder. Below there are some hints on typing in programs and loading them from cassettes. If the program does not work when you type RUN, it probably has a bug (mistake) in it. Some bugs cause the program to "crash" and it stops working. Others cause unexpected things to happen in the program. You can find out about some common bugs on the opposite page.

1 Typing in a listing

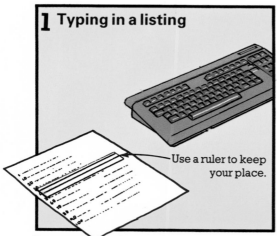

Use a ruler to keep your place.

2

Punctuation and spacing are as important to the micro as letters and numbers, so you have to type in a listing very carefully. Each line will appear on the screen as you type for you to check.

If the program does not work when you try to run it, you can type LIST to display it on the screen. You can then check it again for bugs and correct it before trying again.

1 Loading from a cassette

TV lead

You might see jagged lines on the screen while the program is being loaded.

Cassette port

Cassette lead

2

LOAD "MOUSETRAP"

Try playing the cassette in the usual way to hear how the program sounds.

A program is saved on cassette tape as a series of high-pitched bleeps. To load it into the micro you connect up the cassette recorder as described in the micro's manual. You need to adjust the volume to 7 or 8 and the tone to a high treble setting so the micro can pick up the sounds.

When you type LOAD and the program name in quotes, and press PLAY on the recorder, the program should be copied into the micro. This can take a few seconds or minutes, depending on the length of the program. If the program does not load successfully, the tone and volume settings might need adjusting.

Bugs in programs

This picture illustrates a program which has lots of bugs. The most common bugs are typing mistakes. If you do not type BASIC correctly the micro will not understand the commands. This kind of bug is called a syntax error.

MISSING ". The words after PRINT should be enclosed in quotes.

Most micros send error messages to the screen when they come across something they do not understand. Some do this as you type in the program. Others wait until you RUN or LIST the program. Here are some examples of error messages.

10 PRINT "HOW MANY CROCODILES IN THE RIVER?

20 "YOU HAVE FIVE GUESSES."

SYNTAX ERROR. No PRINT statement to tell the micro to put this on the screen.

30 LET A = 6

40 FOR N = 1 TO 5

50 ONPUT G

SYNTAX ERROR. The word is wrongly spelt so the micro does not understand.

NO SUCH LINE. There is no line 130 in this program.

60 IF G = A THEN N = 5: GOTO 130

CAN'T MATCH FOR. FOR . . TO . . NEXT are part of the same command telling the micro to repeat this and the next four steps five times. It is called a loop. The NEXT part of the command, which should be line 80, has no line number, so the micro does not recognize it.

70 PRINT "WRONG"

NEXT N

90 PRINT "SNAP! YOU HAVE BEEN EATEN UP."

100 END

110 PRINT "RIGHT. NOW PADDLE AWAY FAST!"

120 OK – THAT'S ALL

SYNTAX ERROR. This is not in BASIC so the micro does not understand. It should read END.

Here is the correct program:
```
 10 PRINT "HOW MANY CROCODILES
    IN THE RIVER?"
 20 PRINT "YOU HAVE FIVE GUESSES."
 30 LET A=6
 40 FOR N=1 TO 5
 50 INPUT G
 60 IF G=A THEN N=5: GOTO 110
 70 PRINT "WRONG"
 80 NEXT N
 90 PRINT "SNAP! YOU HAVE BEEN
    EATEN UP!"
100 END
110 PRINT "RIGHT. NOW PADDLE
    AWAY FAST!"
120 END
```

15

Saving programs

After you have typed a program into the micro, you can copy it on to cassette tape. This is useful as the program in the micro's random access memory is lost when it is switched off. You can also save programs on floppy disks, using a disk drive, which is better if you want to store a lot of programs. You can make paper copies with a printer, too.

A cassette recorder, disk drive or printer plugs into a socket on the micro called a port. This contains special circuitry called an interface which converts the micro's own machine code signals into the kind of electrical signals the device uses.

Cassettes

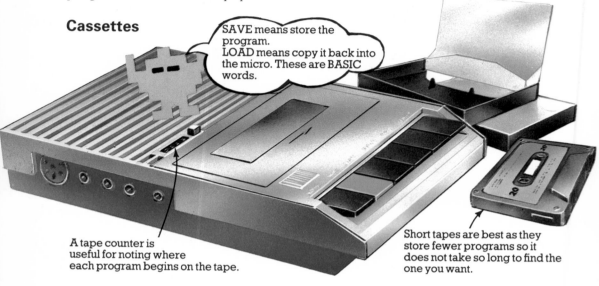

SAVE means store the program.
LOAD means copy it back into the micro. These are BASIC words.

A tape counter is useful for noting where each program begins on the tape.

Short tapes are best as they store fewer programs so it does not take so long to find the one you want.

For most micros you can use an ordinary portable cassette recorder, but a few need their own special recorder. You can buy specially made "data tapes" for recording programs, but any good quality tapes will do.

Saving and loading programs on cassette can be quite tricky. If it does not work, the "recording head" of the recorder may need cleaning. If the program contains bugs, the micro will not let the recorder save it.

1 Saving programs on tape

You connect the cassette recorder to the micro as described in the manual. Make sure the leads do not cross each other or you might get interference.

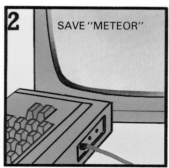

2 SAVE "METEOR"

Then you type SAVE and the program name in quotes on the keyboard and press RECORD and PLAY on the recorder to save the program.

3 As the cassette tape travels past the recording heads on the cassette recorder, the program is saved as a pattern of magnetic dots on the tape.

Printers

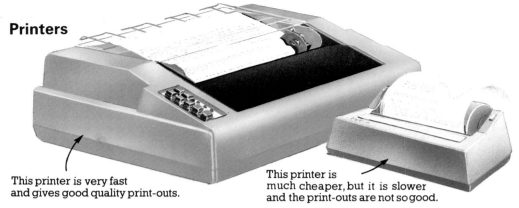

This printer is very fast and gives good quality print-outs.

This printer is much cheaper, but it is slower and the print-outs are not so good.

You can print out program listings, data and sometimes even pictures with a printer which you connect to the micro. Most micros use a standard type of interface called an RS232 inside the connection.

Information saved by a printer is called "hard copy". You can make lots of copies of the same program to distribute among friends. Printers can work very fast. Some expensive ones can print out several lines per second.

Floppy disks

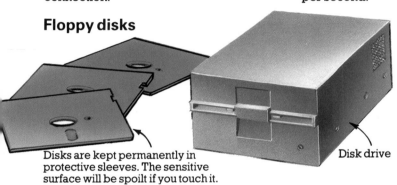

Disks are kept permanently in protective sleeves. The sensitive surface will be spoilt if you touch it.

Disk drive

Read/write head

Disk spinning round in its sleeve.

Floppy disks store programs in the same way as cassette tape. The disk's surface is smooth, without grooves like a record. Saving and loading take place inside a disk drive which you plug into the micro.

The disk is spun inside the disk drive and a "read/write" head moves rapidly over its surface through a slot in the sleeve. This head can "read" any data stored on the disk and "write" new data on to it.

More about saving and loading

When you save a program you usually give it a name. You need to keep a record of program names as, when you want to load a program and you give the micro the name, if a letter or even a space is wrong the micro will not recognize it.

When you load a program back into the micro from tape or disk, a copy goes into the micro's memory. You can then change this copy or use different data without altering the version stored on the tape or disk.

17

Micro pictures

A micro makes pictures by lighting up tiny areas called pixels on the screen. Pictures made by a computer are called graphics and you can give the micro instructions for graphics by typing in a program on the keyboard. You can also make pictures by drawing on the screen with a light pen, or with a special piece of equipment called a graphics tablet. You can find out how these work below.

Lighting up the screen

Pixels

If you look closely at a computer picture you can see all the pixels. Most computers can make colour pictures if they are connected to a colour TV or monitor, and the pictures are made by lighting up areas of pixels in different colours.

Characters (i.e. letters, numbers and symbols) are also made up of pixels. A micro divides the screen up into rows of invisible squares and each character is made by lighting up different combinations of the pixels in a square.

How to make pictures

Pixel
40
30

In a graphics program you tell the micro which pixels to light up by typing in their co-ordinates. The co-ordinates for each pixel show how far it is along and up the screen, measured in numbers of pixels.

Special pen

Graphics tablet

A graphics tablet has a pressure-sensitive surface covered with a grid. You place your picture on the grid, then trace over it with a special pen. This automatically gives the micro the co-ordinates for all the pixels.

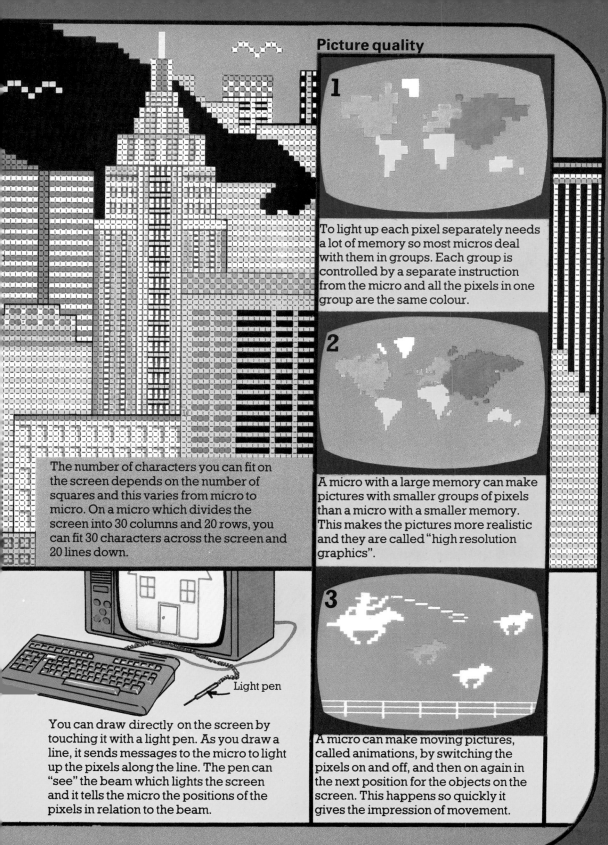

Picture quality

1

To light up each pixel separately needs a lot of memory so most micros deal with them in groups. Each group is controlled by a separate instruction from the micro and all the pixels in one group are the same colour.

2

A micro with a large memory can make pictures with smaller groups of pixels than a micro with a smaller memory. This makes the pictures more realistic and they are called "high resolution graphics".

3

A micro can make moving pictures, called animations, by switching the pixels on and off, and then on again in the next position for the objects on the screen. This happens so quickly it gives the impression of movement.

The number of characters you can fit on the screen depends on the number of squares and this varies from micro to micro. On a micro which divides the screen into 30 columns and 20 rows, you can fit 30 characters across the screen and 20 lines down.

Light pen

You can draw directly on the screen by touching it with a light pen. As you draw a line, it sends messages to the micro to light up the pixels along the line. The pen can "see" the beam which lights the screen and it tells the micro the positions of the pixels in relation to the beam.

19

Micro sound

Most micros can play tunes and make sound effects, and some can even speak words. Micros which can make sounds usually have a special chip called a synthesizer inside the keyboard. For some micros you can buy a synthesizer unit separately.

You can tell the micro which sounds to make by typing in a command such as SOUND or BEEP, followed by numbers indicating the note you want (e.g. C or B) and how long you want it to be played. You can find out how the micro makes sounds in this picture.

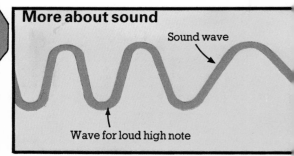

Your instructions to the micro.

MICRO

Micro's message to the synthesizer.

Electric signal from the synthesizer.

SYNTHESIZER

1 Making music

You can buy music programs on cassette – some programs make screen pictures at the same time.

You can program a micro to play a tune by giving it instructions for each note. Some micros can also play chords and harmonies. These have several "voices" which can each be programmed to play different notes at the same time.

2

Another way to tell the micro which notes to play is with a light pen. You give the micro a program which makes a stave (the lines for musical notes) on the screen, then draw the notes you want with a light pen.

When you type in an instruction for a sound the micro sends a message to the synthesizer in machine code, telling it which sound to make. The synthesizer produces an electric signal which is strengthened in an amplifier and then sent

More about sound

Sound wave

Wave for loud high note

The vibrations in the air made by a loudspeaker are called sound waves, and different sounds have different shaped waves. For instance, a loud, high note has tall, squashed-up waves. The height of the waves shows how loud the note is. The

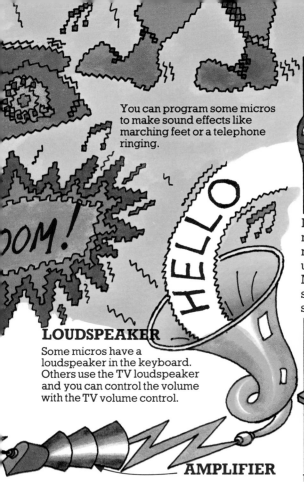

You can program some micros to make sound effects like marching feet or a telephone ringing.

LOUDSPEAKER

Some micros have a loudspeaker in the keyboard. Others use the TV loudspeaker and you can control the volume with the TV volume control.

AMPLIFIER

on to a loudspeaker. The signal makes the loudspeaker vibrate and this makes the sound. Different signals from the synthesizer make the loudspeaker vibrate at different rates and this makes different sounds.

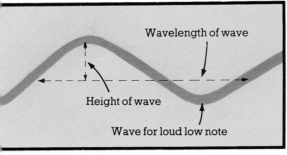

Wavelength of wave

Height of wave

Wave for loud low note

wavelength of the waves, that is, how close together they are, shows how high or low the note is (this is called the pitch). The variations in the volume and pitch of a sound over a period of time is called the sound envelope.

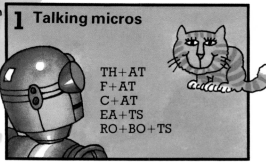

1 Talking micros

TH+AT
F+AT
C+AT
EA+TS
RO+BO+TS

It is more difficult for a micro to speak than make music as the sounds in words are more complicated. Most words are made up of several sounds, e.g. RO-BO-TS. Micros which can talk have the word sounds stored in machine code in a special chip.

WH+ATS
YO+UR
NA+ME

Using a synthesizer, the micro puts the word sounds together to make words, according to grammar rules stored in its memory. This is called speech synthesis. Micros with speech synthesizers are useful for blind people who cannot see a screen, or children who cannot read.

This town ain't big enough for both of us.

It is much more difficult for computers to understand speech. They have to be programmed to recognize all the word sounds. As people have different voices and pronounce words differently, only a computer with a huge memory can store enough information.

Inside the keyboard

The picture on these two pages shows the parts inside a small computer. All computers have the same basic parts as those shown here, although most are more complicated and have more components.

The most important parts in the computer are the chips – the four black boxes on legs. All the work inside the computer is done by electrical signals pulsing through the chips and flowing along the metal tracks on the printed circuit board. You can find out more about how the computer works on the next few pages.

ROM chip
The permanent program of instructions telling the computer how to operate is stored in here.

Voltage regulator
This converts the 9 volts from the power supply into the smooth, regular 5 volts which the micro uses.

Printed circuit board (PCB)
This has metal tracks laid out on its surface and the electrical signals in the computer flow along the tracks between the chips. There are other electronic components on the board called capacitors and resistors and these help control the flow of electricity.

Resistors

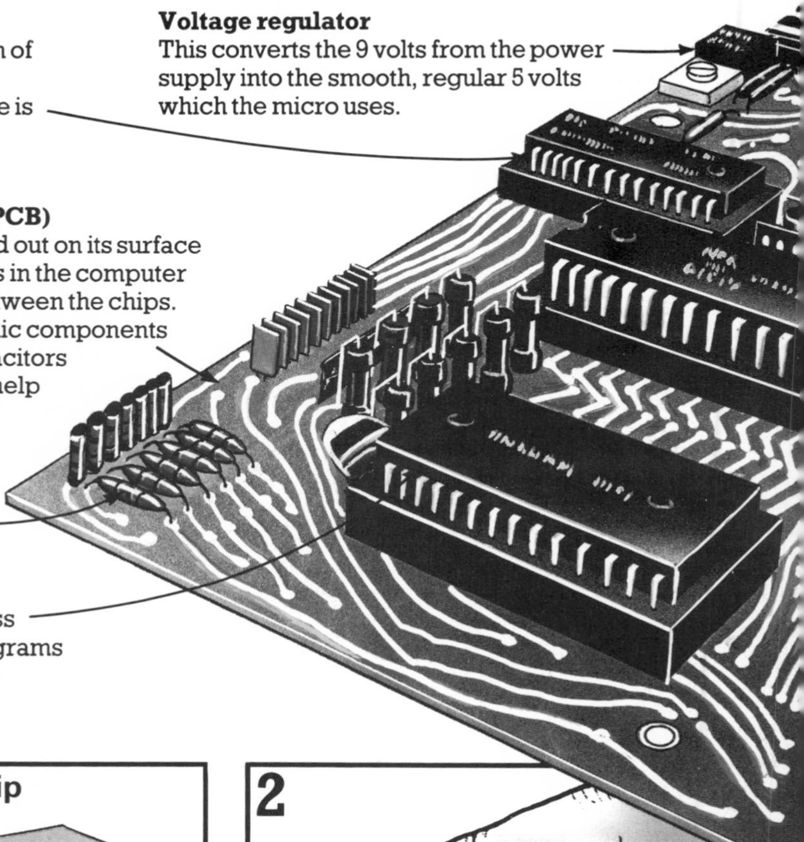

RAM chip
This is the random access memory, where the programs and data you put into the computer are stored.

1 Looking at a chip

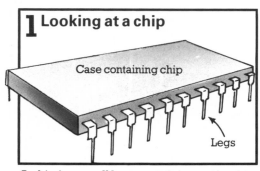

Case containing chip

Legs

A chip is a small box containing a tiny chip of silicon. The surface of the chip is covered with further circuits which are minute and very complicated. The metal legs on the chip's case carry electrical signals to and from the chip.

2

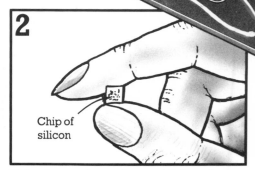

Chip of silicon

This picture shows the actual size of a chip. It is about as thick as a fingernail and may have as many as ten different circuits engraved in it. The proper name for a chip is "integrated circuit" or IC.

Sinclair Computer Logic chip

This is a special chip which contains extra operating instructions for this computer.

Sockets for connecting the TV and power supply and for other equipment such as cassette recorder or printer.

Modulator

This converts the computer's signals into signals the TV can understand.

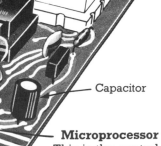

Capacitor

Microprocessor

This is the central processing unit (CPU), the control centre of the computer. It carries out the instructions in your program and controls the flow of information to the RAM and TV screen. It contains a quartz crystal "clock" which pulses over a million times a second and regulates the flow of electrical signals inside the computer.

Edge connector

This is where you plug in equipment such as an add-on memory pack or program cartridge. Metal strips at the edge of the board carry electric signals to and from the memory or cartridge.

The circles show where the metal tracks pass through the printed circuit board and continue on the other side.

More powerful computers

1

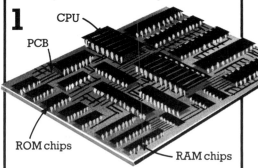

CPU

PCB

ROM chips

RAM chips

More powerful computers have larger memories and more chips. The picture shows the PCB of another micro with about 40 chips on it. There are several ROM and RAM chips and this gives the micro a larger memory.

2

Cabinets

A really powerful computer, such as those used by large companies, has hundreds of PCBs covered with chips. The PCBs are stored in cabinets and all the cabinets may fill a room. This is called a mainframe computer and it can carry out many tasks at the same time.

3

A minicomputer is a smaller version of a mainframe. It has several cabinets with PCBs and it is usually specially designed to do one particular kind of work, such as accounting or storing the information for a databank.

Inside a chip

Each of the chips in a computer has circuits specially designed for the particular jobs it has to do. The picture on the right shows two silicon chips, much enlarged. One is a microprocessor and the other is a ROM chip and you can see the patterns of the different circuits on each chip. The circuits are so small and intricate that when they are tested during manufacture up to half of them have to be discarded because they are faulty.

Microprocessor ▶

A microprocessor is sometimes called a computer on a chip. It has several different kinds of circuits and in fact can do the work of a tiny computer. The microcomputer is named after the microprocessor.

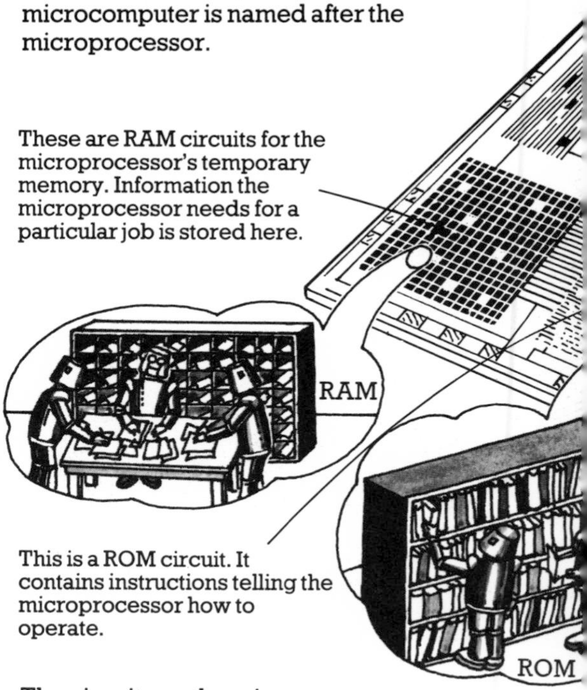

These are RAM circuits for the microprocessor's temporary memory. Information the microprocessor needs for a particular job is stored here.

RAM

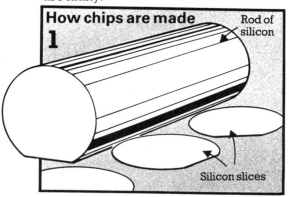

How chips are made

1

Rod of silicon

Silicon slices

This is a ROM circuit. It contains instructions telling the microprocessor how to operate.

ROM

Chips are made from very pure silicon crystal. The crystal is shaped into rods and then cut into slices about 100mm in diameter and 0.5mm thick. Each slice will make about 500 chips. Silicon is made by purifying sand, and so the chips are quite cheap.

The circuits on the microprocessor are connected by tracks called "busses". Tracks which continue on to the printed circuit board to connect the microprocessor to other chips are also called busses.

2

Circuit design

Light pen

3

Slices of silicon

Nowadays computers help to design circuits for chips. Here, a light pen is being used to make alterations to a circuit design. Next it will be reduced in size to fit on a chip.

The circuit designs are placed on the chips by a photographic process and the slices of silicon are put in a furnace. There, the circuits are chemically etched into the silicon.

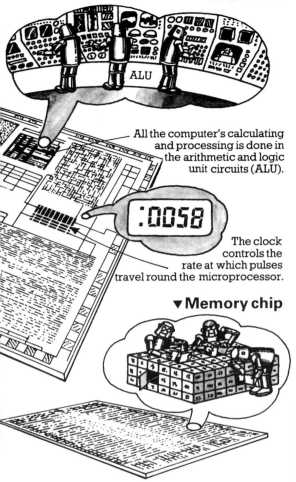

All the computer's calculating and processing is done in the arithmetic and logic unit circuits (ALU).

The clock controls the rate at which pulses travel round the microprocessor.

▼ Memory chip

The circuits on a memory chip are like hundreds of little boxes. On a ROM chip, each box contains a piece of information, but on a RAM chip the boxes are empty until you put the information in.

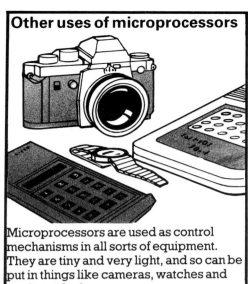

Microprocessors are used as control mechanisms in all sorts of equipment. They are tiny and very light, and so can be put in things like cameras, watches and pocket calculators.

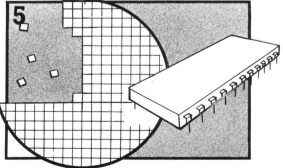

Microprocessors have replaced old-fashioned, bulky electronic devices in many everyday things such as washing machines and telephone switchboards. They are more efficient and reliable.

Probes

4

Many different circuits can be etched into the same chip, and the process can take several weeks. The finished chips are tested on the slice with tiny probes under a microscope, and faulty ones marked.

5

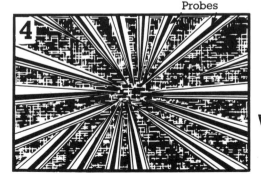

The silicon slices are then cut up into individual chips with a diamond saw and the faulty ones thrown away. The perfect chips are then packaged into protective cases which can be fastened on to a PCB.

How chips work

The circuits in a chip contain thousands of tiny components called transistors through which the current flows in rapid pulses. Some of the transistors are combined to form "gates". Some gates allow pulses through and some do not. This creates patterns of pulse signals and "no-pulse" signals, which make up machine code. The no-pulse is just as important as the pulse signal.

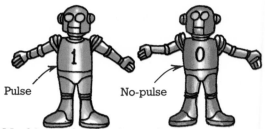

Pulse   No-pulse

Machine code is made up of only two signals – pulse and no-pulse. Codes made up of two signals are called binary codes. The signals are represented by 1 and 0. Below you can see how binary works.

Counting in binary

8s 4s 1s 2s

$(1 \times 8) + (1 \times 4) + (0 \times 2) + (1 \times 1) = 13$
13 is written as 1101 in binary.

Binary numbers are made up from two digits, 0 and 1. They are written in columns of ones, twos, fours, eights, and so on. You make up the numbers by putting 1s and 0s in the correct columns.

1000s 10s 1s 100s

$(4 \times 1000) + (0 \times 100) + (2 \times 10) + (1 \times 1) = 4021$

The decimal counting system we use works on the same principle as binary, but we use ten digits (0 to 9), probably because we have ten fingers. Decimal numbers are written in columns of ones, tens, hundreds, and so on.

More about machine code

One bit

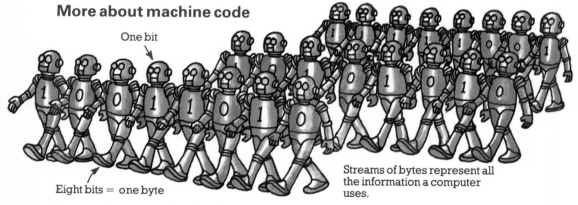

Eight bits = one byte

Streams of bytes represent all the information a computer uses.

Each pulse or no-pulse signal is called a "bit", short for binary digit. Most micros use groups of eight bits to represent pieces of information. A group of eight bits is called a "byte" and is rather like a word made up of eight letters.

There are 256 different ways of arranging the 0s and 1s in an eight-bit byte. This is enough to represent each symbol on the keyboard by a single byte, with some left over for things like colours and sounds.

How the computer processes information

The computer processes information by sending the pulse signals which make up machine code bytes through different combinations of transistors, called gates. These alter the patterns of the pulses they receive in a particular way. The points where they receive signals are called terminals. Some gates receive two signals but only send on one. Here are three kinds of gate:

An AND gate sends a pulse on if it receives one at both its terminals.

An OR gate sends a pulse on if it receives one at both or either of its terminals.

A NOT gate has one terminal. It only sends a pulse on if it does not receive one.

How the computer adds up

These pictures show how the computer uses a particular arrangement of gates to add up any binary digits (1+1, 1+0, 0+1, 0+0). The computer does all its processing using sets of gates like this, though this is a very simple example.

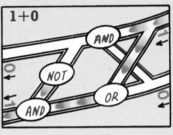

1+0

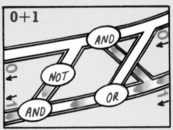

0+1

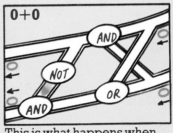

0+0

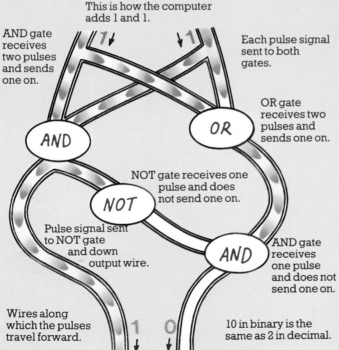

This is how the computer adds 1 and 1.

AND gate receives two pulses and sends one on.

Each pulse signal sent to both gates.

OR gate receives two pulses and sends one on.

NOT gate receives one pulse and does not send one on.

Pulse signal sent to NOT gate and down output wire.

AND gate receives one pulse and does not send one on.

Wires along which the pulses travel forward.

10 in binary is the same as 2 in decimal.

This is what happens when other binary digits are added together in the same set of gates.

27

More about chips

The way a micro works depends on the kind of chips it has inside it. Micros with the same microprocessor understand the same version of machine code. The interpreter which translates BASIC into machine code is stored in the ROM. Micros with the same ROM chip usually understand the same dialect of BASIC. This is known as software compatibility.

BASIC is more like human language than machine code, so the micro needs a large interpreter. Languages like BASIC are called high-level languages. Low-level languages are more like machine code, and are easier for the computer to translate.

Microprocessor chips

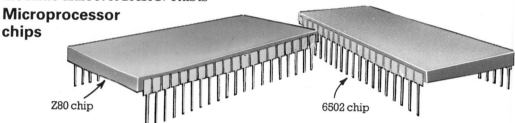

Z80 chip   6502 chip

There are lots of different kinds of microprocessors, but the two most commonly found in home micros are the Z80 and 6502 chips shown here. The differences between them lie in their circuitry, so it might be difficult to tell them apart just by looking at their outside cases. The micro's operating instructions stored in the ROM chip have to be written in the correct version of machine code, for instance, in Z80 machine code for the Z80 microprocessor.

Inside the ROM

The ROM consists of tiny areas with number addresses which each store one byte of information. You can ask a micro to show you the bytes stored in some areas by typing PEEK and an address. The manual will tell you which addresses you can PEEK into. The byte will appear on the screen as a decimal number.

MONITOR   INTERPRETER

The special program which handles the running of a micro, called the monitor, is stored in the ROM along with the interpreter. One of the monitor's tasks is to detect which key on the keyboard has been pressed. It receives an electrical signal from the key and refers to a keyboard map to find which byte represents that key. Most micros conform to ASCII (American Standard Code for Information Interchange) for which bytes represent which symbols.

Inside the RAM

System variables	This area contains information for the micro, such as where the next character will appear on the screen.
Program area	This is where the program is stored.
Display file	The micro puts a machine code copy of what is displayed on the screen here.
Variables	This is where data is stored.
Current line and work space	This contains the line being typed.
Calculator stack	The CPU does some of its sums here.
Spare area	This is free space for you to use, or for other RAM areas to "borrow" if they get full.
Machine stack	The CPU uses this area for storing things, such as program line numbers.
GOSUB stack	The program line number the micro must return to after being sent on a diversion is stored here.

The RAM is divided into areas storing different kinds of information. You can PEEK into RAM in the same way as you can into ROM. You can also change the bytes stored in some areas of RAM by typing POKE followed by an address and a number. (You cannot do this with ROM as it is a permanent memory.) The micro's manual will tell you which areas of RAM you can POKE without interfering with its other jobs. You can usually POKE into the "system variables" area, and you can store things in the spare area, and retrieve them with PEEK.

Low-level programming

If you program a micro in machine code, it can act on the instructions immediately, without first having to translate them. This is useful in fast games programs, for example. Programming in streams of binary digits is complicated, though, so you can use other low-level codes, such as hex or mnemonics, instead. These are like fast, shorthand versions of machine code.

One byte

Decimal value of group is 13 – called D in hex.

Hex equivalent to the byte is D5.

Mnemonic codes
MPY = multiply
STO = store
ADD = add

Hex, short for hexadecimal, is a number system based on 16 digits – 0 to 9, and A to F which represent the numbers 10 to 15. An eight-bit byte can be written as two hex digits. You divide the byte into two groups of four binary digits, and turn each group into a single hex digit.

A mnemonic code is a set of abbreviations which stand for certain instructions to the micro. Each mnemonic sets off a particular chain of activity in the micro. Low-level codes are easier for the computer to convert into machine code, so the interpreter can be smaller.

The story of the micro

The first true electronic computers were built in Britain in World War II. Unlike earlier mechanical adding machines, they were programmable and had memories. These computers were used by scientists to crack enemy codes and plot the flight paths of shells. Information about them was kept top secret for many years.

When peace came, a few big business corporations and governments began to use computers, but no one else could afford them. Since then, computers have got smaller, cheaper and more powerful. This has led to the development of the micro, which is a computer anyone can use – not just scientists.

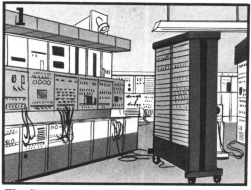

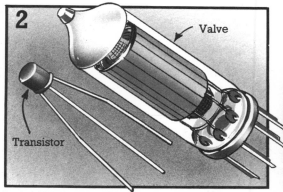

The first computers were built before transistor switches were invented. They used valves instead. These were about seven centimetres high and made of glass, and there were about 18,000 in a computer. They frequently failed, and teams of engineers were needed to locate dud valves in the complicated circuits.

In the 1950s transistors were invented in the USA. They did the same job as valves, but were smaller, cheaper and faster. Valve manufacturers lost their scientists to new transistor companies. Soon transistors were replacing valves in all kinds of electronic equipment, such as radios, as well as computers.

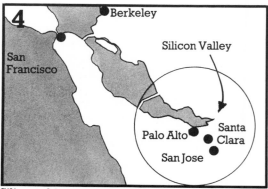

By the 1960s, the US government was competing in the space race and needed small, powerful computers for their spacecraft. They financed research into "integrated circuits", which were a new invention and consisted of several transistors combined in a tiny sliver of silicon, nicknamed a chip.

Silicon chips were an enormous breakthrough, and led to a new science called microelectronics. The main centre of research was the Santa Clara Valley in California, which became known as Silicon Valley. Microelectronics engineers learnt how to pack more and more components on to the same chip.

Computer generations

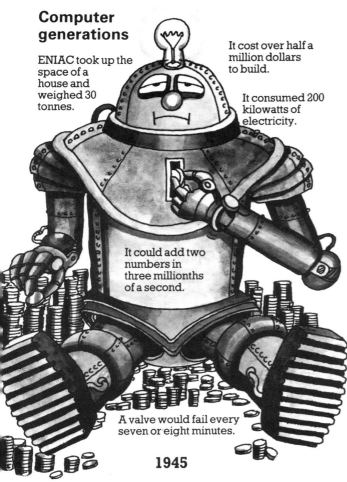

ENIAC took up the space of a house and weighed 30 tonnes.

It cost over half a million dollars to build.

It consumed 200 kilowatts of electricity.

It could add two numbers in three millionths of a second.

A valve would fail every seven or eight minutes.

1945

The history of computers can be divided into four generations, each smaller and more powerful than the last. Huge valve computers were the first generation. One of these was called ENIAC. It was completed in 1945 after taking two years to build. The second generation used transistors. Computers with chips were the third generation and the invention of microprocessors and further miniaturisation brought the fourth.

A chip is smaller and thinner than a contact lens.

It costs under five dollars.

It can add two numbers in one ten-millionth of a second.

It almost never breaks down.

It consumes only a tiny amount of electricity.

1980

---

5 Microprocessor chip

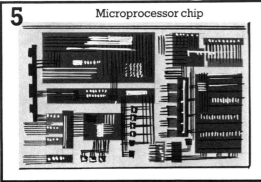

A major breakthrough came in 1971 when it became possible to place all the main electronic parts of a computer on to one chip. This was called a microprocessor. A computer circuit that would once have filled a whole room with thousands of valves could now be contained in a 5mm square silicon chip.

6

This new technology led to the production of microcomputers, which a small business or even a single person could afford. Micros were on the market by the late 1970s. Now you can buy a micro the size of a book which costs as little as a few of the valves contained in one of the earliest computers.

31

Computer chains

You can link a micro to another computer anywhere in the world, provided they have the necessary connections and there is a way of transmitting the signals between them clearly. They can use existing means of communication, such as telephone lines and satellites. The computers usually need special programs to help them understand each other, as they might use different languages or dialects, or work at different speeds. People link computers together to share information or programs. Anything in one computer's memory can be copied into another.

Using networks

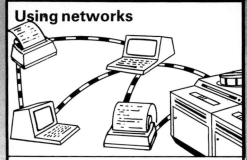

Computers can be linked together in "nets", or networks, usually using a telephone. You can find out how to do this on this page. You need a password to tell the other computer to receive your messages. You can link up with any computer equipment, for example, lots of micros could share the same printer.

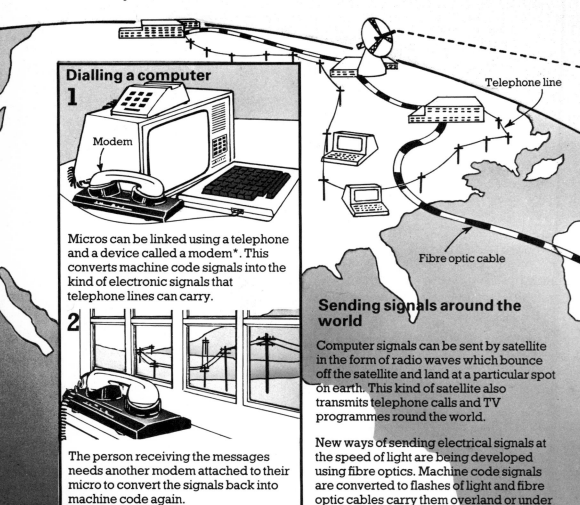

Dialling a computer

1

Modem

Micros can be linked using a telephone and a device called a modem*. This converts machine code signals into the kind of electronic signals that telephone lines can carry.

2

The person receiving the messages needs another modem attached to their micro to convert the signals back into machine code again.

Telephone line

Fibre optic cable

Sending signals around the world

Computer signals can be sent by satellite in the form of radio waves which bounce off the satellite and land at a particular spot on earth. This kind of satellite also transmits telephone calls and TV programmes round the world.

New ways of sending electrical signals at the speed of light are being developed using fibre optics. Machine code signals are converted to flashes of light and fibre optic cables carry them overland or under the sea to anywhere in the world.

*Modem stands for modulator/demodulator.

SUPERMARKET SEAFOOD
FRESH TODAY

1. SQUID   1.10 PER KG
2. PRAWNS   0.60 PER KG
3. MUSSELS   0.70 PER KG

You could do your shopping by computer, and in the future you probably will. You link a micro to a shop's computer and a display of goods for sale appears on the screen. You type in your order and give your bank account number. The shop's computer arranges delivery and contacts your bank to charge your account.

DEAR JOHN,
  PERHAPS YOU WOULD LIKE TO EXPLAIN YOUR BEHAVIOUR WITH THAT BOWL OF SOUP

Micros linked by telephone can be used as an electronic mail system. Instead of writing a letter and posting it you can type it out on your micro's keyboard, dial a connection with someone else's micro and leave the letter on the screen. This is much quicker than using ordinary mail.

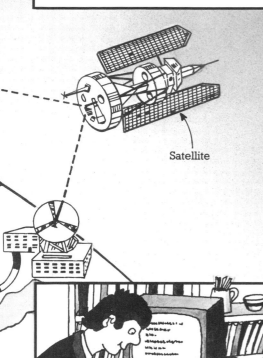

Satellite

Business people can work at home using a micro in a network to communicate with a central computer in their office. They will have access to files and be able to send messages to colleagues in the network.

Nowadays, more and more micros are being connected to computerized information centres called teletext systems. With a worldwide network of computers storing and exchanging information, you can have almost any knowledge at your fingertips.

Already in some schools, micros on the pupils' desks are connected up to a central one. The teacher uses this to keep in touch with what each pupil is doing and to supply programs. The pupils can work at their own speed.

Micro control

Most micros can control other electrical equipment as easily as they control their own screen or printer, provided they have the right "ports", or sockets where you plug the equipment in. The micro's machine code signals must be converted into a form the equipment can use. This conversion usually takes place at the control port on the micro's keyboard. The part which does the controlling is the microprocessor.

Running a model railway

Here is a railway circuit controlled by a micro, which is connected to the track by a lead from the control port. It sends signals to the track to change the points and stop and start the train.

Getting signals in and out

You plug the connecting lead into the control port.

The micro needs a way of sending signals out to whatever it is controlling, and of getting progress reports back. The control port contains the interface* which handles this information. If your micro does not have a control port, you can usually buy one for it.

The micro controls the speed of the train by varying the amount of power sent to it. It will also count the number of times the train goes round the track and can be programmed to stop it after a certain number.

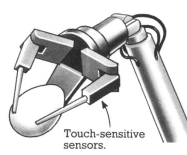

Touch-sensitive sensors.

The micro can use sensors to tell it what is happening, for instance, if it needs to know the position of something it has to move. A robot arm controlled by a micro might have touch-sensitive areas to tell it when it contacts something, or it might have a light-sensitive "eye".

1 Robots

You can turn some micros into robots by connecting a special metal "arm", and programming the micro to make it move and pick things up. The microprocessor in the micro acts as the "brain" of the robot, using messages from sensors in the arm to help work out the next move.

*The connection which passes information between the micro and what it controls.

Micro controlling
the railway.

Control port

Sensor

Points

Sensor

Points

When the train crosses a pressure-
sensitive sensor, a message is sent to the
micro telling it which part of the track the
train is on and which set of points it is
approaching. The micro has a program
telling it what to do next.

Micros in space

The Space Shuttle carries a
microcomputer similar to an ordinary
home micro. Unmanned interplanetary
probes like the Viking and Voyager
missions to Mars and Saturn were
controlled by micros on board linked
by radio to large computers on earth.

These micros carry out complicated
calculations very quickly. They plot
courses and control engine thrust and
fuel consumption. They can monitor
experiments and supervise
photography. They radio reports to
Earth and receive instructions back.

Larger robots are used in factories. They
do lots of jobs, from moving heavy car
bodies about to putting together tiny
mechanical parts. These are robots and
not just machines because they can be
programmed to do different things and
can make some of their own decisions.

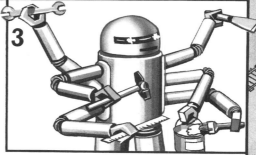

"Robot" is the Czech word for worker. It
was first used to describe artificial men by
the Czech playwright Karel Capek in the
1920s. Robots can be used for boring or
dangerous jobs. They do not breathe, so
they can work in space or in mines where
there are poisonous gases.

Other micro users

Micros are used for all kinds of jobs. They are small and powerful and can work on any information once it has been converted into machine code. They process information and calculate much faster than a human. They can store lots of information in a small space, and have totally accurate memories, unlike humans.

Micros are often used for analysing data. They store sets of information and compare it to input data.

Micros in medicine

DOES YOUR HEAD HURT?
YES
IS YOUR VISION AFFECTED?
YES
HAVE YOU EVER HAD MIGRAINE?
NO

As well as keeping medical records, some doctors use micros to help with their diagnoses. A patient types in answers to questions and the micro compares them to lists in its memory. It gives possible diagnoses and cures.

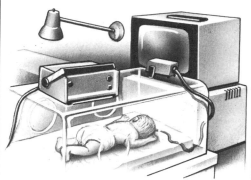

Staff at the Hammersmith Hospital in London developed a micro-based system to care for premature babies who have difficulty breathing and need their lungs artificially inflated. Too much air forced in can damage the lungs. Too little can cause brain damage. The micro monitors a baby's lungs so it gets just enough oxygen.

Weather forecasting

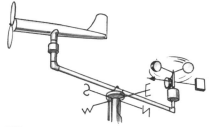

Microcomputers at local weather stations process data received from instruments, and send the results to a central meteorological office.

Helping the disabled

People who cannot speak or hear can use micros to communicate. There are special keyboards for semi-paralysed people which require only a slight movement of a finger or some other part of the body to select a word or letter.

Computer-aided design

A micro can show objects in 3-D and rotate them so the designer can look at them from another angle. An architect designing a bridge or a building can ask the micro to calculate stresses and decide if it would be safe.

Portable micros

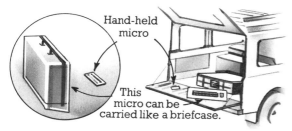

Hand-held micro

This micro can be carried like a briefcase.

People doing field work, like a geologist prospecting for oil, or a building site foreman, might use a portable micro. It can store and process facts on the spot.

Brewing beer

Barley malt

Micros are used in automated breweries and other factories. Making beer involves mixing and fermenting at precise temperatures for set times. Sensors tell the micros when one stage is complete and another ready to begin.

Learning with micros

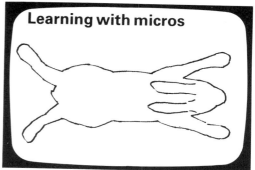

Micros are used to teach anything from French to navigation. You can even "dissect" a rabbit on the screen using a light pen instead of having to cut up a real animal.

Micros in business

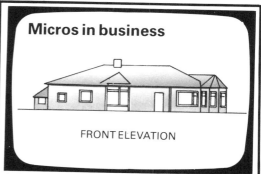

FRONT ELEVATION

Self-employed people and small businesses can use a micro to keep track of accounts and invoices. A freelance architect or designer could also use the graphics on a micro.

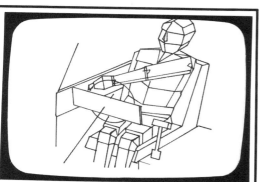

A small space like the front of a car needs to be designed so that the driver can reach all the controls and has enough room. A designer can buy a special program which draws people on the screen. They can be moved about to see if they fit into the design.

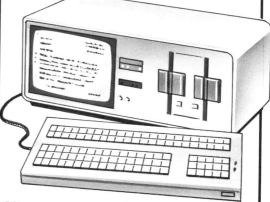

Microcomputer wordprocessors are used in offices to cut down on typing and paperwork. Standard letters and documents are typed and corrected on a wordprocessor and then stored on disk to be printed out when needed.

Adding to your micro

Once you are familiar with your micro and what it can do, there are lots of things you can buy to add to it. Extra equipment such as disk drives, printers, and graphics pads are called peripherals. To connect something to the micro you need an interface to convert the signals between the two, and different pieces of equipment need different interfaces. A micro usually has interfaces for a cassette recorder and TV built into it. Many also have interfaces for a printer, disk drive or light pen. If not, you can buy a separate one. Many peripherals, especially printers, plotters and modems (for telephone linkage to other computers) use a standard interface called an RS232. If you want to add several peripherals to the micro, you can buy a "motherboard" into which you can slot boards or cards containing interfaces for different equipment.

Extra memory

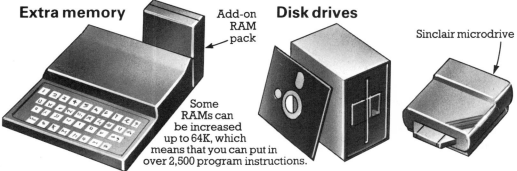

Add-on RAM pack

Some RAMs can be increased up to 64K, which means that you can put in over 2,500 program instructions.

You may want to increase your micro's RAM size before you buy any peripherals. You can then use longer programs for more exciting games and better graphics. You can buy add-on RAM packs for some micros. These are cartridges containing RAM chips which slot into the micro to connect with the PCB. Other micros have space on the PCB for extra RAM chips to be fitted by a dealer.

Disk drives

Sinclair microdrive

If you want to store long programs, or lots of information in a home database, you will find a disk drive much quicker than a cassette recorder. They are far more expensive, though. Disk drives for home micros usually use minifloppy disks which measure about 13.5cm across. The Sinclair microdrive uses even smaller disks, called microfloppies. They store 100K each, which is about enough space for all the words in this book.

Joysticks and paddles

Joystick   Fire button   Paddle

Joysticks and paddles are useful for playing arcade-type games where you want to move things like aircraft and spaceships around the screen. You can use keys on the keyboard for this, but joysticks and paddles give you more control and are more fun to use. With a joystick you can move the object in any direction, but paddles only move it up, down, left and right. Usually joysticks have a "fire" button on them to fire missiles. Many home micros have built-in interfaces for joysticks.

Graphics

If you are interested in graphics, you can produce exciting pictures on the screen by drawing on a graphics pad. You can also get good quality "hard copy" pictures using a plotter. A pen is supported over a sheet of paper and the movement of the pen is controlled by the computer's program. These are expensive pieces of equipment, though, so you could buy a light pen instead which is much cheaper.

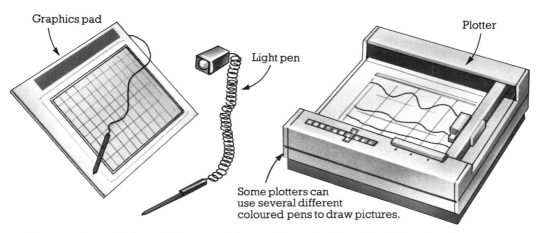

Graphics pad

Light pen

Plotter

Some plotters can use several different coloured pens to draw pictures.

You can buy a high-resolution graphics card or cartridge for some micros to improve the picture quality. As well as providing more colours, it makes the groups of pixels you can control smaller, so details can be finer. It might make characters smaller, too, so you can fit more lines of text on the screen. High-resolution graphics use up a lot of memory, so you may need more RAM as well.

More about printers

There are three main types of printer – thermal, dot matrix and daisy-wheel. Thermal printers are the cheapest, and though the print can be rather messy they are adequate for printing out programs. Dot matrix printers are also quite cheap. Daisy-wheel printers are expensive, but give very good quality print. Bi-directional printers print one line going forward and another going back to save time.

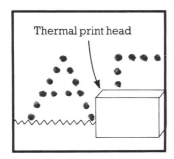

Thermal print head

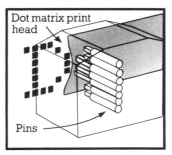

Dot matrix print head

Pins

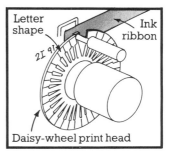

Letter shape

Ink ribbon

Daisy-wheel print head

Thermal printers send out little sparks on to heat-sensitive paper, which turns black where a spark hits it. Patterns of black dots form letters.

Dot matrix printers have a print head consisting of lots of pins. Letters are formed by combinations of pins shooting out and making dots on the paper.

The print head on a daisy-wheel printer looks like a bicycle wheel without a rim. On the end of each "spoke" is a character shape.

Buyer's guide

On the next few pages there are descriptions of some of the main home computers currently available. They are arranged roughly in order of price with the least expensive models first.

If you are new to computers, the jargon used to describe them is very confusing at first. If you are buying your first computer, though, there are only a few main features you need be concerned with and these are outlined in the descriptions on the next few pages. At the bottom of this page there are some explanations to help you understand some of the terms used.

The best way to find out about the different computers is to ask friends who own computers about their machines or go along to a computer user's group and talk to the people there. You can also read the reviews in computer magazines and ask lots of questions in computer shops. (Ask the assistant to explain any terms you do not understand.) Before you buy your computer, think carefully about what you want to use it for and decide how much you want to spend. If you decide to buy a simple, inexpensive machine, check how much extra memory you can add and whether you can also use it with other equipment such as a disk drive or printer, etc. If you become a keen computer hobbyist, you will soon find you outgrow the simplest version of the computer and will want to add to it.

Processor This is the microprocessor, the CPU of the micro. The specifications for a micro usually tell you which processor the micro uses. The two main processors are the 6502 and the Z80 (see page 28). If you are buying your first micro you need not really worry about this.

Keyboard Most micros have a keyboard like an electric typewriter. A few, though, have touch sensitive keys which do not move when you press them. Typing in programs on a touch sensitive keyboard takes a bit longer than on one with keys which move.

Most micros have the same arrangement of letters as on a typewriter. This is called a QWERTY keyboard. (QWERTY is the sequence of letters in the first row of letters on a typewriter.) Sinclair computers (see opposite) have a special system where each key carries a programming word as well as a letter. This means you do not have to type in the programming words letter by letter.

Screen display The number of characters (i.e. letters and symbols) that the micro can display on the screen is measured in columns for the number of characters across the screen and lines for the number of lines of text which will fit down the screen. Some micros have automatic scrolling – when the screen is full the text automatically moves up the screen to make space at the bottom.

Graphics Picture quality is measured by the number of points you can plot across and down the screen. This is called screen resolution.

Interfaces Most micros have built-in interfaces for a TV and/or monitor and for a cassette recorder. They may also have interfaces for some of the following: printer, disk drive, joysticks, Prestel and for networking (linking up with other computers). If a micro does not have the interface you want you can usually buy one separately.

Software This is all the programs for a micro on cassette, disk or in printed form. The software for one micro does not work on another micro unless they are related machines like the Sinclair ZX81 and Spectrum.

ZX81 (Sinclair)

Z80A processor
1K RAM expandable to 16K
32 column × 24 line screen display
63 × 43 screen resolution

The ZX81 is a small, inexpensive microcomputer. It has a touch sensitive keyboard with the Sinclair keyword system – each key carries a programming word so you do not have to type in the words letter by letter. It uses a TV set for display and an ordinary cassette recorder for saving and loading programs. It can make only a black and white display. It also has a built-in interface for the Sinclair printer.

The ZX81 is the world's biggest selling microcomputer and there is probably more software for it than for any other computer. Most of the programs are games programs on cassette or printed in books and magazines.

ZX Spectrum (Sinclair)

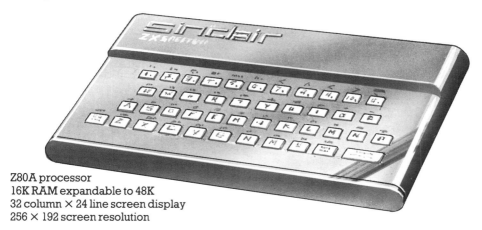

Z80A processor
16K RAM expandable to 48K
32 column × 24 line screen display
256 × 192 screen resolution

The ZX Spectrum is less than twice the price of the ZX81, but it has a much larger memory. It has the same keyword system for entering programming words as the ZX81, but its keys move when you press them. It can also make colour pictures and sounds.

It uses a colour TV set for display and an ordinary cassette recorder for saving and loading programs. It also has interfaces for the Sinclair printer and for a microdrive. This is a small disk drive for saving and loading programs on microfloppy disks. You can also add an RS232 and a networking interface to this micro.

It can make pictures with eight colours and sounds of over ten octaves. It has an internal loudspeaker but only one sound channel so you can only play one note at a time.

Most software produced for the ZX81 works on the Spectrum, but there are also lots of programs written specially for it.

41

Jupiter Ace (Jupiter Cantab)

Z80A processor
3K RAM
32 column × 24 line screen display.
256 × 192 screen resolution

This small, inexpensive microcomputer uses the programming language FORTH instead of BASIC. It has a calculator type keyboard, good graphics and sound, but no colour. It is the first home computer to use FORTH so there is very little software and most of the books on how to program in FORTH are quite complex. It has a printer interface and a microfloppy disk drive.

Oric 1 (Oric Products International)

6502A processor
16K RAM expandable to 48K
40 column × 28 line screen display
240×200 screen resolution

Inexpensive microcomputer with a calculator type keyboard, sixteen colours and four sound channels. It has a Centronics printer interface. A more expensive version of the same computer is available with 48K RAM.

VIC 20 (Commodore)

6502 processor
5K RAM expandable to 29K
22 column × 23 line screen display
176 × 158 screen resolution

This is a small, sturdy home computer with colour graphics and sound. It uses a colour TV set for display, but needs a special VIC cassette recorder for storing and loading programs. There are lots of programs available on cassette and cartridge, and printed in magazines.

On the standard machine you can produce graphics in 16 colours using the symbols on the graphics keys. To produce graphics with DRAW and other BASIC graphics commands you need a special graphics program cartridge. For sounds the VIC uses the TV loudspeaker and can make four different sounds at the same time.

It also contains built-in interfaces for the following equipment: a disk drive, printer, joysticks, light pen and there is also an RS232 interface cartridge.

PC1500 (Sharp)

CMOS processor
3.5K RAM expandable to 7K
26 character display in one line
7 × 156 screen resolution
dimensions 20.5cm × 9cm

This pocket sized microcomputer can be powered by batteries or the mains so you really can take it anywhere. It has its own built-in black and white liquid crystal display screen. To load and save programs on cassette you can use an ordinary cassette recorder, but you need a special interface unit which the computer fits into. This interface also works with the Sharp printer which can print in four colours. The small screen makes it not really suitable for games.

Electron (Acorn)

6502 processor
32K RAM
This is a new computer and some of the technical specifications were not released when this book was published.

The Electron is a small colour computer made by Acorn, the company who produce the BBC micro. It has a QWERTY keyboard with moving keys and uses the same version of BASIC as the BBC micro, so most BBC programs also work on the Electron.

TI-99/4 (Texas Instruments)

9900 processor
16K RAM expandable to 48K
29 column × 24 line screen display
256 × 192 screen resolution

The TI-99/4 uses a TV set for display and can make pictures in 16 colours. It also has good music and sound effects, using its own internal loudspeaker. It can play three notes at once, over five octaves. You can also buy a separate speech synthesizer which can pronounce over 200 words.

The TI-99/4 uses an ordinary cassette recorder for saving and loading programs and there is lots of software on cassette, cartridge and disk. Other extra equipment for this micro includes a printer, disk drive, joysticks and an RS232 interface.

Dragon (Dragon Data)

6809 processor
32K RAM expandable to 64K
32 column × 16 line screen display
256 × 192 screen resolution

This is a small micro designed for home use. It has a keyboard with moving keys and uses a TV set for display and an ordinary cassette recorder. It has good colour graphics using nine colours, and can make a wide range of sounds using one sound channel and the TV loudspeaker. Additional equipment for the Dragon includes a printer, disk drive, joysticks, and RS232 and Prestel interfaces.

Atari 400 (Atari)

6502 processor
16K RAM
40 column × 24 line screen display
320 × 192 screen resolution

The Atari 400 has a flat, touch-sensitive QWERTY keyboard. It uses a TV set for display, but needs its own cassette recorder for loading and saving programs from cassette. Much of the software for this machine, though, is in cartridges which slot straight into the micro. There is a wide range of good games programs for the Atari 400 and you can buy joysticks as an optional extra. Other additional equipment includes a disk drive and printer and the micro has 16 colours for graphics and four sound channels.

TRS-80 Colour Computer (Tandy, or Radio Shack in the U.S.A.)

6809E processor
16K expandable to 32K
32 column × 16 line screen display
256 × 192 screen resolution

The TRS-80 Colour Computer uses a colour TV set for display and an ordinary cassette recorder for saving and loading programs. It has eight colours and can also make sounds. Additional equipment for the Colour Computer includes joysticks, a printer, a disk drive and an RS232 interface.

Colour Genie (EACA)

Z80 processor
16K RAM expandable to 32K
40 column × 24 line screen display
196 × 96 screen resolution

The Colour Genie has many similarities to the Tandy computers. It can run Tandy software listings with minor alterations, but not the cassettes. It has a typewriter type keyboard and printer, disk drive, light pen, joystick and RS232 interfaces.

Lynx (Camputers)

Z80A processor
48K RAM expandable to 192K
40 column × 24 line screen display
248 × 256 screen resolution

This micro has a typewriter type keyboard and eight colour graphics and sound. It is an expandable system with a disk drive, printer and other add-ons.

Atom (Acorn)

6502 processor
2K RAM expandable to 12K
32 column × 16 line screen display
256 × 192 screen resolution

The Atom is a small hobby or home business computer. It uses a TV set for black and white display, but you can buy an extra PCB to make colour graphics. It uses an ordinary cassette recorder. Additional equipment for the Atom includes a disk drive, printer, joysticks and a network and Prestel interface.

Newbrain (Grundy)

Z80A processor
32K RAM expandable to 2Mbytes
40 or 80 column × 25 line screen display
640 × 250 screen resolution

One of the main features of this computer is the extent to which the memory can be expanded by adding plug-in memory modules. It has no colour or sound facility, but the black and white graphics are very clear. It is designed for expansion and has a number of sockets for attaching a printer, modem and expansion board and networking interface. There is a variety of mainly business orientated software available in ROM cartridges.

BBC Micro (Acorn)

6502 processor
16K RAM expandable to 32K
40 column × 32 line screen display
320 × 256 screen resolution (Model A)

The BBC micro comes in two versions, the Model A which is the basic version and Model B, a more advanced system. The Model A can be upgraded to Model B level and the complete system with all the available peripherals makes a powerful small computer.

It uses an ordinary TV set and cassette recorder and has eight colours and three sound channels. Additional equipment available for the BBC micro includes a disk drive interface, network interface, speech synthesizer, program cartridge interface, paddles, printer and Prestel interface. There is extensive software of all kinds.

Commodore 64 (Commodore)

6502 processor
64K RAM
40 column × 25 line screen display
320×200 screen resolution

The Commodore 64 has the same keyboard layout as the VIC 20, but a much larger memory and a standard size screen display. It has good graphics with sixteen colours and three sound channels. The 64 can use most of the PET and VIC software and also has a good range of business and games cartridges of its own. There is a disk drive and modem interface and a plug-in cartridge which makes it compatible with PET peripherals.

HX-20 (Epson)

6301 processor
16K RAM expandable to 32K
20 column × 4 line screen display
120×32 screen resolution

This micro has a small, neat keyboard with a built-in screen, printer and micro-cassette recorder. It can also be connected to a TV or monitor and can work off batteries or the mains. Additional equipment for the HX-20 includes ROM cartridges, a barcode reader, acoustic coupler for linking to another computer via the telephone, and an RS232 interface.

Atari 800 (Atari)

6502 processor
16K RAM expandable to 48K
40 column × 24 line screen display
320 × 192 screen resolution

Similar to the Atari 400 but has a proper keyboard and expandable memory. The 800 can use the same range of cartridge software as the 400, which includes games, home and business programs and extra programming languages.

PET (Commodore)

6502 processor
16K RAM expandable to 96K
40 column × 25 line screen display
512 × 512 screen resolution

The PET was one of the first "personal computers", that is, a computer designed to be used by one person. It has a built in monochrome screen and needs a Commodore cassette recorder which may also be built into the micro.

The PET is used mainly by serious computer hobbyists and by businesses and schools. Additional equipment for the PET includes a disk drive and printer and it has a built-in PET IEEE-488 interface (this is an alternative to the RS232 interface). There is an extensive range of educational, business and games software on cassette or disk.

Apple II Plus (Apple)

6502 processor
16K expandable to 48K
40 column × 24 line screen display
280 × 192 screen resolution

The Apple, like the PET, is used by serious computer hobbyists, small businesses and schools.

The basic machine has a motherboard with a number of slots into which you can fit PCBs for various different functions, e.g. for memory expansion and PCBs which enable you to use other programming languages.

Other additional equipment includes a printer, graphics tablet, disk drive and Prestel interface. There is a lot of educational, business and games software for the Apple, in printed form and on disk.

Buyer's Guide chart

	Processor	RAM size	Screen display columns × lines	Graphics resolution
ZX81 (Sinclair)	Z80A	1K — 16K	32 × 24	63 × 43
ZX Spectrum (Sinclair)	Z80A	16K — 48K	32 × 24	256 × 192
Jupiter Ace (Jupiter Cantab)	Z80A	3K	32 × 24	256 × 192
Oric 1 (Oric Products International)	6502A	16K — 48K	40 × 28	240 × 200
VIC 20 (Commodore)	6502	5K — 29K	22 × 23	176 × 158
PC1500 (Sharp)	CMOS	3.5K — 7K	26 × 1	7 × 156
Electron (Acorn)	6502	32K		
TI-99/4 (Texas Instruments)	9900	16K — 48K	29 × 24	256 × 192
Dragon (Dragon Data)	6809	32K — 64K	32 × 16	256 × 192
Atari 400 (Atari)	6502	16K	40 × 24	320 × 192
TRS-80 Colour Computer (Tandy or Radio Shack, USA)	6809E	16K — 32K	32 × 16	256 × 192
Colour Genie (EACA)	Z80	16K — 32K	40 × 24	196 × 96
Lynx (Camputers)	Z80A	48K — 192K	40 × 24	248 × 256
Atom (Acorn)	6502	2K — 12K	32 × 16	256 × 192
Newbrain (Grundy)	Z80A	32K — 2Mbytes	40/80 × 25	640 × 250
BBC Micro (Acorn)	6502	16K — 32K	40 × 32	320 × 256
Commodore 64 (Commodore)	6502	64K	40 × 25	320 × 200
HX-20 (Epson)	6301	16K — 32K	20 × 4	120 × 32
Atari 800 (Atari)	6502	16K — 48K	40 × 24	320 × 192
PET (Commodore)	6502	16K — 96K	40 × 25	512 × 512
Apple II Plus (Apple)	6502	16K — 48K	40 × 24	280 × 192

Micro words

Animations   Moving pictures on the screen.

Arithmetic and logic unit (ALU)   The circuits in the central processing unit where calculations and comparisons are carried out.

ASCII   American Standard Code for Information Interchange. A standard way of representing letters and numbers with eight-bit binary numbers.

Backing store   Programs or data saved outside the computer on tape or disk.

BASIC   A general-purpose programming language suitable for most kinds of programs. The letters stand for Beginners' All Purpose Symbolic Instruction Code. Most micros use BASIC.

Baud rate   A measurement of the speed at which one bit travels from one part of the computer to another, or between a computer and a peripheral, for instance a cassette recorder. One baud is one bit per second.

Binary   A counting system using only two digits (0 and 1). Machine code is a binary code.

Bit   One of the two digits (1 and 0) that make up binary code. In a computer, a bit is a pulse signal (1) or a no-pulse signal (0).

Bug   A mistake in a program.

Bus   Tracks along which data is moved about the computer.

Byte   Most micros work with groups of eight bits at a time, called a byte.

Central processing unit (CPU)   The circuits which control all the other parts of the computer and where calculations are carried out.

Character   A number, letter or symbol.

Chip   A tiny slice of silicon with lots of electronic circuits etched into it. They are kept in protective cases. Chips are used in computers to do all the work.

Compatibility   Computers are said to be compatible if they can understand the same programs.

Data   Any information you give the computer which will be worked on according to the instructions in a program. The information and results from a computer are also called data.

Database   An organised file of information held in the computer's memory or on tape or disk.

De-bugging   Finding mistakes in a program and correcting them.

Dialect   There are several versions of BASIC, called dialects, which use slightly different commands.

Error message   A message the computer flashes up on the screen to tell you that there is a bug in the program, and sometimes what kind of bug it is and where it is.

Fortran   A high-level programming language used mainly by scientists and mathematicians.

Gate   An arrangement of transistors which works on the pulses travelling through the circuits of a computer. All the computer's processing is done using gates.

Graphics   Pictures made with a computer.

Hard copy   Programs or data printed out by the computer using a printer.

Hardware   A computer, or a piece of related equipment, such as a disk drive or printer.

Hex   A counting system based on 16 digits (0 to 9 and A to F). It is useful for low-level programming as an eight-bit byte can be expressed as two hex digits.

Input   Any information or instructions you feed into the computer.

Integrated circuit (IC)   Minute electrical circuits containing thousands of electronic components on a tiny chip of silicon.

Interface   Special circuits which convert the signals from a computer into a form other electronic equipment can deal with, and vice versa. Different pieces of equipment need different interfaces.

Interpreter   A special part of the computer's permanent memory (ROM) where instructions in a programming language (usually BASIC in a micro) are converted into machine code.

Kilobyte (K)   One kilobyte is 1024 bytes.

Listing   A program written, typed or printed out on paper.

Load Put a program into a computer's memory from cassette tape or disk.

Machine code The pattern of electronic pulse signals which the computer uses to do all its work.

Microprocessor A chip containing all the different kinds of circuitry a computer needs to control an electronic device. The CPU of a microcomputer is a microprocessor chip.

Mnemonics A code consisting of abbreviated instructions. Mnemonics are used as an aid to low-level programming.

Modem Short for modulator/demodulator. A device which converts the signals from a computer into a form which can travel down telephone lines.

Monitor Part of the ROM which holds instructions telling the CPU how to operate.

Motherboard A circuit board into which you can slot other PCBs.

Network A system of computers, sometimes with other computer peripherals, linked together to share information.

Output Any information the computer gives you.

Pascal A high-level programming language for general use.

PCB See Printed circuit board.

Peripherals Equipment that you can attach to a computer, such as extra screens, printers or plotters.

Pixels Tiny areas on the screen which the computer can switch off or on to make the shapes for letters or pictures.

Port A socket on a micro where you plug in a lead connecting it to another piece of equipment.

Printed circuit board (PCB) The board inside a computer which holds all the chips and other components. It has metal tracks on it to carry the electrical signals between the components.

Program A numbered list of instructions to make the computer do a particular job.

Programming language A language in which a program of instructions for a computer must be written. There are lots of different languages. High-level languages consist of words and symbols and are easier to use than low-level languages which resemble machine code more closely.

Random access memory (RAM) Chips where any information you give the computer is stored. You can retrieve or change this information. The RAM chips empty of stored information every time the computer is switched off.

Read only memory (ROM) All computers have ROM chips which store instructions telling them how to work. The instructions are built into the ROM chips when they are made, and the information in ROM is permanent.

Save Store a program outside the computer, usually on tape or disk.

Screen resolution The number of pixel groups on the screen which the computer can control. High resolution graphics are detailed pictures made by a computer which can control lots of small groups of pixels. Low resolution graphics are pictures made with fewer, larger groups of pixels.

Sensor A device outside a computer that measures light, pressure or temperature and sends information back to the computer.

Software Computer programs.

Syntax error A bug in a program due to a mistake in the programming language.

Synthesizer A piece of equipment or circuitry which produces musical notes or sounds through a loudspeaker.

System variables An area of RAM which stores information about different parts of the computer, for instance, where the next character will be printed on the screen, and the addresses of the boundaries between different areas of RAM. These can shift depending on how much is stored in each area.

Transistor An electronic component which stops or sends on the pulses in the circuits of a computer, depending on the pulses it receives. A single chip contains thousands of transistors.

Visual display unit (VDU) A screen, similar to a TV screen, designed specially for a computer.

Index